Food and Festivals

THE CARIBBEAN

Linda Illsley

RAINTREE
STECK-VAUGHN
PUBLISHERS
A Steck-Vaughn Company

Austin, Texas

Food and Festivals

THE CARIBBEAN

Other titles:

The Caribbean ● China ● India
Mexico ● West Africa

Cover photograph: Selling fruit at a market in Jamaica

Title page: Traditional dancers in Jamaica

Contents page: Drinking the sweet milk of a coconut

Published by Raintree Steck-Vaughn Publishers, an imprint of Steck-Vaughn Company

Printed in Italy. Bound in the United States.
1 2 3 4 5 6 7 8 9 0 03 02 01 00 99

Library of Congress Cataloging-in-Publication Data
Illsley, Linda.
The Caribbean / Linda Illsley.
    p.   cm.—(Food and festivals)
Includes bibliographical references and index.
Summary: Discusses some of the foods enjoyed in the Caribbean region and describes special foods that are part of such specific celebrations as Christmas and New Year, Carnival, the Crop Over harvest festival, and Phagwa.
ISBN 0-8172-5758-6
1. Festivals—Caribbean area—Juvenile literature.
2. Cookery, Caribbean—Juvenile literature.
2. Food habits—Caribbean area—Juvenile literature.
3. Caribbean area—Social life and customs—Juvenile literature.
[1. Cookery, Caribbean. 2. Food habits—Caribbean area. 3. Caribbean area—Social life and customs]
I. Title. II. Series.
GT4823.I55 1999
394.1'09729—dc21   98-36014

CONTENTS

The Caribbean and Its Food

USA

ATLANTIC OCEAN

The Caribbean

The Caribbean's place in the world

N

Nassau

BAHAMAS

Havana

CUBA

TURKS and CAICOS ISLANDS

GREATER ANTILLES

CAYMAN ISLANDS

DOMINICAN REPUBLIC

LEEWARD ISLANDS

Kingston

HAITI

VIRGIN ISLANDS

JAMAICA

PUERTO RICO

ANGUILLA

HISPANIOLA

St. CROIX   SABA

BARBUDA

ANTIGUA

St. KITTS and NEVIS

MONTSERRAT   GUADELOUPE

CARIBBEAN SEA

DOMINICA

MARTINIQUE

LESSER ANTILLES

St. LUCIA

DUTCH ANTILLES

BARBADOS

WINDWARD ISLANDS

0   400 km

ARUBA

0   200 miles

St. VINCENT and the GRENADINES   GRENADA

TOBAGO

TRINIDAD

SOUTH AMERICA

4

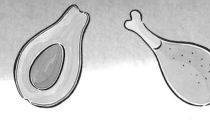

SUGARCANE

Sugarcane was introduced to the Caribbean by Europeans. The juice of the sugarcane is used to make sugar, rum, and a refreshing, sweet soft drink.

RICE

Rice is grown all over the Caribbean. It is one of many different foods that were brought to the Caribbean by Indian settlers.

FRUIT AND NUTS

Because of the hot Caribbean climate many different tropical fruits can be grown on the islands.

VEGETABLES

Root vegetables, such as yams and sweet potatoes, are an important part of the Caribbean diet. They were brought to the Caribbean from Africa.

FISH AND SEAFOOD

The Caribbean Sea is rich in fish and seafood, such as lobsters and crabs. Fish is cooked in many different ways.

SPICES

Ginger, nutmeg, peppers, and allspice are grown in the Caribbean. They add flavor to many Caribbean dishes.

People, Food, and Farming

Once sugarcane has been harvested, it goes to factories to have the sweet juice crushed out of it.

The Caribbean is a region made up of over 30 large islands in the Caribbean Sea, between North and South America. It is in the tropics, so the climate is warm all year.

The people of the Caribbean are a mixture of many different cultures. The first people to live there were Arawak Indians. Then, about 500 years ago, people from Spain, England, France, and Holland settled in the Caribbean. They brought slaves from Western Africa to work on sugar and tobacco plantations. More recently, East Indians, Chinese, and Arabs have settled there.

Each of these groups of people brought with them their traditional celebrations, their cooking, and sometimes even the ingredients, which became part of the diet of Caribbean people.

Rice and bread

Rice and bread are very important in the Caribbean. Rice is used in dishes such as rice and peas, and with Indian curries and Chinese dishes.

Rice grows well in the tropical Caribbean climate because it needs rain and sunshine. During most of the year the temperature stays between 75° F (24° C) and 85° F (29° C). There is a rainy season between September and November.

There are many kinds of bread in the Caribbean, but the most famous is the *dhalpourri*. This is a flat Indian bread made with ground split peas. It is filled with curried potatoes, meat, and chickpeas and is rolled up and eaten like a sandwich.

▲ A rice harvest in Cuba

Once rice has ▶ been picked, it is sifted to get rid of the husks, or shells, around each grain.

7

Tropical fruit

Caribbean people buy their fruit from large open markets. Some of the fruits, such as bananas, coconuts, and mangoes, are sold abroad.

Coconuts are very popular in the Caribbean. The "milk" or juice inside is a refreshing drink and the kernel itself is used as an ingredient in many different dishes such as cakes, curries, desserts, and sauces.

UNUSUAL FRUITS

You can see some Caribbean fruits, such as bananas and pineapples, in your local stores. But others are more unusual. Breadfruit has bumpy, pale-green skin and a creamy flesh. Ackee has an orange skin with a bright yellow fruit. It is the main ingredient of the national dish of Jamaica, ackee and saltfish.

In the warm climate of the Caribbean tropical fruits like pineapples and watermelons grow all year round.

In 1789, there was mutiny on the HMS *Bounty*, an English ship taking breadfruit plants to the Caribbean. The breadfruit plants had been gathered in Tahiti and were being taken to the Caribbean to be planted there. The sailors were furious because the captain, William Bligh, used their precious drinking water on the breadfruit plants. They set him adrift in an open boat and took over the ship.

▲ Breadfruit trees can grow as tall as 60 ft. (18 m). Although breadfruit is a fruit, it is often cooked like a vegetable and used instead of potatoes or rice.

▼ Vegetables in the Caribbean come in all kinds of shapes, sizes, and colors.

Vegetables

Lots of different vegetables grow in the Caribbean. Many of the islanders grow vegetables just for themselves, but much is sold abroad.

Vegetables are cooked in hundreds of different ways. Caribbean cooks often mix both sweet and savory ingredients in their food. Sweet potatoes are sometimes cooked in sugar (see recipe on page 19), or mashed. Yams are cooked like potatoes. Cassava can be made into a kind of flour or eaten as a vegetable. Callaloo is like spinach and is used in a dish called pepperpot soup.

Seafood

People in the Caribbean can choose from seafood such as clams, lobster, tuna, snapper, shark, conch, and mullet. Seafood is used in festival foods as well as everyday dishes. It is barbecued, curried, or cooked in the traditional Caribbean style of "jerk." Jerk fish, beef, or chicken is made by flavoring the fish or meat with a peppery sauce and then barbecuing it.

▲ Barbecued fish

▼ Fishing is an important industry in the Caribbean.

Brightly colored spices are bought by weight from open-air markets and stores throughout the Caribbean.

Spices

Wherever you go in the Caribbean, spices are usually used to flavor food. The mixture of spices varies from island to island. In Trinidad, people use *massala* in their dishes. This is a mixture of coriander seeds, anise, cloves, cumin, fenugreek, peppercorns, mustard and turmeric. Peppers are among the most famous spices used in Caribbean cookery. Pepper sauces are made from hot, yellow peppers that grow all over the islands, and each cook has a different way of preparing the sauce.

HISTORY THROUGH FOOD

Caribbean dishes can tell you about the history of the islands. For example, *foo-foo, coo-coo* and *dunckunoo* (dishes made from plantain and okra) came from West Africa. Escaviche fish (raw marinated fish) is found in islands that were Spanish colonies, and *fricassee de poulet au coco* (chicken in coconut milk) is cooked on islands that were French.

11

Caribbean Religions

There are many different religions in the Caribbean. Most people are Christians—mainly Roman Catholic or Anglican. There are also many people who follow versions of African religions, such as Voodoo, Pocomania, and Santeria. However in the Caribbean, these religions have been mixed with Christianity. In some countries, like Guyana and Trinidad, many people follow the Hindu and Muslim religions.

▲ During the Santeria festival of Shango, beautifully prepared food is laid out on an altar as a religious offering.

◀ For these churchgoers in Barbados, the visit to church is social as well as religious.

Festivals and food

The food and festivals of the Caribbean reflect the many different religions and cultures. A festival might be a Muslim celebration such as Id-ul-Fitr, which marks the end of Ramadan. But the food that is served can be any style, from Chinese to Brazilian! The one thing common to all Caribbean cooking is the use of fresh ingredients.

RASTAFARIANISM

In Jamaica, a religion called Rastafarianism forbids its followers to eat pork or fish without scales. Many Rastafarians are vegetarian or vegan. *Ital* food is a vegetarian type of cooking introduced by Rastafarians. It includes things like vegetable patties and is now becoming popular in the Caribbean.

This Rastafarian family in Jamaica wears the red, green, and gold colors of their religion. The man is also wearing the dreadlock hairstyle that many Rastafarians wear.

▲ At this Hindu wedding in Trinidad, the bride is wearing a traditional red *sari*. Offerings of food, such as rice, are made to Hindu gods throughout the ceremony.

Food and celebrations

Food is an important part of most religious celebrations in the Caribbean. Voodoo followers, when asking for a favor from a spirit or "Iwa," make offerings of cake and grilled corn. In a traditional Hindu wedding, only vegetarian food is served, but in Christian weddings it is common to eat meat dishes, such as curried lamb. There is a recipe for curried lamb on the opposite page.

◀ Curried lamb, with a selection of spices

Curried Lamb

INGREDIENTS

1 Tablespoon olive oil

1 pound lamb, cut into cubes

2 large onions, sliced finely

2 teaspoons curry powder

1 Tablespoon freshly grated coconut or dried coconut

$1/2$ teaspoon allspice

$2 1/4$ cups canned chicken or beef broth

1 bay leaf

Pinch of cayenne pepper

Salt and a dash of Tabasco sauce

Ask an adult to heat the oil in the saucepan. Add the meat and fry for about five minutes. Take it out and put into a bowl.

In the same pan, fry the onions until soft. Stir in the curry powder, allspice, and coconut and cook for a few minutes.

Add the broth, bay leaf, cayenne pepper, and the fried meat. Cover and simmer for two hours.

Taste and add salt if needed. If using Tabasco sauce, stir in just before serving.

Be careful when frying. Ask an adult to help you.

Christmas and New Year's

▼ Many of the traditions of Christmas that we know in America, such as a visit from Santa Claus, are also popular in the Caribbean.

Christmas and New Year's are celebrated all over the Caribbean. This is the season of bamboo bursting, when bamboo poles are filled with gunpowder and snapped like firecrackers. Lots of special dishes are prepared.

Ham, turkey, or a whole roasted pig or goat are some of the traditional Christmas foods served on many of the islands. Caribbean people also eat a Christmas cake very similar to plum pudding, but flavored with rum.

SCOTTISH FOOD

Another European Christmas recipe is *jug jug*, which is a kind of pastry filled with pork and beef. It is said originally to have come from Scotland.

Professional dancers in the ▶ Caribbean putting on a traditional dance for tourists. Dancing is an important part of Christmas celebrations.

Jonkonnu and Papa Jab

Christmas and New Year's are also marked by parades. Pipes, cowbells, whistles, foghorns, and drums announce the arrival of the Jonkonnu (or John Canoe) dancers. The dancers are dressed in different costumes as animals, kings, and funny characters, and their dancing pattern tells stories that have been passed down from one generation to the next.

Papa Jab is a folk character from St. Lucia. During the New Year celebrations, someone dresses up as Papa Jab and joins groups of people in masks and costumes, singing and dancing through the streets. Children are scared of Papa Jab because legend has it that he will eat badly behaved children!

Candied sweet potatoes are a favorite dish in the Caribbean. There is a recipe for this dish on the facing page.

HAPPY NEW YEAR

In Jamaica, according to tradition, to make sure you have a good year, the first thing that you eat in the New Year should be roasted suckling pig.

Candied Sweet Potatoes

INGREDIENTS

4 sweet potatoes, peeled

Peel of 1 orange, grated

2 Tablespoons butter

3 Tablespoons brown sugar

1 cup of water

EQUIPMENT

2 saucepans   Baking dish, greased

Chopping board   Colander

Wooden spoon   Oven mitts

Knife   Grater

Turn the oven on to a medium temperature. Ask an adult to boil the potatoes for about 10 minutes. Drain and allow to cool. Cut into thick slices.

Grate the orange peel and put it in the second saucepan with the butter, sugar, and water. Cook over a low flame, stirring constantly for five minutes, or until the sugar has melted and the mixture has thickened.

Arrange the sweet potatoes in the baking dish. Pour the orange syrup over them, making sure they are all coated evenly.

Put the dish in the oven and bake for 30 minutes or until browned. Ask an adult to take the potatoes out of the oven.

Always use oven mitts to take hot dishes from ovens. Ask an adult to help you.

Carnival

Carnival began as a Christian festival. It originally took place just before Lent, when certain foods, such as meat, were forbidden. This is how the festival got its name—the word "carnival" comes from the Latin words *"carne levare,"* which means "to take away meat."

The sound of steel drums is probably the most famous sound in the Caribbean. Steel drums were invented in Trinidad.

French settlers introduced Carnival to the Caribbean several hundred years ago. Later, it was celebrated by African slaves. At carnival time the slaves tried to forget how hard their lives were. They made fun of their masters by dressing up and copying them.

In the Caribbean, Carnival is still a time for dancing, playing music, and dressing up. Each costume is carefully designed, and a King and Queen of the carnival are chosen from hundreds of masked people.

Costumes are decorated with satin, beads, feathers, and plastic, and they are made using wonderfully patterned materials. Some costumes are traditional to particular islands, such as the She Devil costume of Martinique, or the 20-ft. (6-m) Mocko Jumbies of St. Thomas.

Preparations for Carnival take months. Clothes and models have to be made and tried out so that everything is perfect for the big event.

▲ Carnival parades are usually long, and it takes the carnival-goers hours to make their way through the streets.

▼ Fried chicken is sold all over the Caribbean, and each family has a different mixture of spices to season the flour. Some like it spicy, while others like it plain.

Party time

Carnival is celebrated on most of the islands and at different times of the year. In Curacao it takes place in January, while in Antigua it is in late July. The most famous carnival is in Trinidad and Tobago. It starts at 4 A.M. on the Monday before Ash Wednesday and continues for 48 hours! During this time thousands of people march and dance in the streets to the rhythm of steel bands. There are stands where delicious food, such as fried chicken, *rotis* filled with chicken or stewed beef, and vegetable fritters, is sold.

Sweet treats

Many of the foods sold at carnival time are very sugary. Candy and cake made with coconut and honey are sold at roadside stands.

Tamarind balls are made of sugar, salt, and tamarind fruit, and they have a tangy flavor. *Bulla* is made using ginger grown on the islands. It is a sweet cake that is a real favorite of children, especially in Jamaica.

▲ Sorrel drink is a refreshing carnival drink. It is made from dried sorrel flowers mixed with water, ginger, orange juice, and sugar.

Drinks are sweet, too. There is a green drink made from sugarcane, which is very refreshing. Chilled coconut milk is also popular.

◄ Coconut milk is best drunk straight from the shell.

Children's Carnival

In Trinidad and Tobago there is a children's carnival, which is just as colorful and exciting as the main carnival. Children dance and take part in competitions to see who is wearing the best costume.

Children love taking part in Carnival because it's a good opportunity for singing, dancing, and having fun.

Fried Chicken

INGREDIENTS

4 pieces of chicken   Salt and pepper
2 eggs   Oil
$2/3$ cup flour

EQUIPMENT
Sieve
Bowl
Plate
Frying pan
Whisk

Crack the eggs into a bowl and beat them well with the whisk.

Add a pinch of salt and pepper to the flour and then sift the mixture onto the plate.

Dip each of the chicken pieces into the beaten egg. Then roll them in the flour. Ask an adult to heat up enough oil in a frying pan to cover the chicken completely.

Once the oil is hot, ask an adult to add the chicken pieces one by one. Cook until they are brown on the outside and white on the inside.

Ask an adult to do the frying. Hot oil can be very dangerous.

Food and Harvest Festivals

Some festivals in the Caribbean celebrate the harvest of crops or other food.

In St. Lucia, a fishing festival is held every year on Saint Peter's Day, which is on June 29. Fishermen give thanks to Saint Peter and Saint Paul. Their brightly painted fishing boats and boat sheds are blessed, and there is a special mass. "Saltfish" cakes are a favorite dish.

▲ Saltfish cakes are a favorite dish at festival time. There is a recipe for them on page 29.

◄ Colorful fishing boats in the fishing village of Anse le Raye, in St. Lucia

Crop Over

Many islands have a festival called Crop Over. This is a harvest festival that was started by slaves to celebrate the end of the sugarcane harvest.

Barbados has the most famous Crop Over. There are fairs, concerts, cart parades, and other activities, including a calypso competition and the crowning of the Calypso King.

▼ Crop Over festival in Barbados is celebrated with special stilt dancing.

Phagwa

Phagwa (pronounced 'pag-wa') is a Hindu festival that is celebrated in Guyana and Surinam. It was brought to Trinidad in the Caribbean by Indian settlers, and is similar to the Indian festival of Holi.

Phagwa, like Holi, is a spring festival that is held near the full moon in March. It celebrates the arrival of spring and the new growth of crops and flowers.

In Trinidad, people go to parks and throw or spray colored powder on each other. They dance and sing folk songs and religious songs.

These girls are celebrating Phagwa in Trinidad.

Saltfish Cakes

EQUIPMENT

Food processor
Large saucepan
Plate
Frying pan

INGREDIENTS

$^1/_2$ lb. saltfish (dried, salted cod)
3 potatoes, peeled and boiled
1 onion, chopped
1 clove garlic, chopped
1 egg
2 Tablespoons scallions, chopped
1 teaspoon fresh parsley, chopped
Pepper to taste
3 Tablespoons flour
Oil

Wash the fish and soak it in cold water overnight. Cover with fresh water and boil for 10 minutes. Once it has cooled, remove the skin and bones.

Put the fish, potatoes, onion, garlic, scallions, parsley, egg, and pepper into a food processor and mix well.

Take a handful of the mixture at a time and press it into small cakes. Once you have used all the mixture, coat each fish cake with flour.

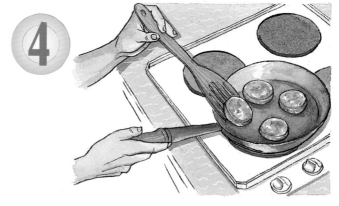

Ask an adult to heat some oil in a frying pan and fry the fish cakes for about 8 minutes, until they are golden brown.

Always be careful with frying. Ask an adult to help you.

Glossary

Anglican   A member of the official Church of England.

Ash Wednesday   The first day of Lent.

Calypso   A kind of music that comes from the West Indies.

Christians   People who believe in the religion based on the teachings of Jesus.

Colonizers   People who go to settle in other countries.

Cutting   A piece cut from a plant.

Id-ul-fitr   A Muslim ceremony that marks the end of Ramadan.

Fasting   Giving up eating and drinking.

Fertile land   Land that is good for growing crops.

Hinduism   The main Indian religion based on the belief that God has many forms.

Hurricane   A very strong storm that causes a lot of damage.

Mocko Jumbies   Dancers from St. Thomas who stand on stilts that make them 20 ft. (6 m) high.

Muslim   A person who follows the Islamic religion that believes in one God, Allah.

Rastafarianism   A religion from Jamaica that involves the worship of the old emperor of Ethiopia, Ras Tafari, as God.

Roman Catholicism   The Christian Church that is led by the Pope.

Roti   A flat, Indian bread.

Sari   A piece of clothing from India. It is a long piece of cloth that is wrapped around the body like a dress and worn by women.

Vegan   A person who does not eat meat, fish, or any animal products such as dairy products.

Vegetarian   A person who does not eat meat or fish.

Photograph and artwork acknowledgments
Andes Press Agency 5 (top right), p7 (top); Axiom Photographic Agency 5 (middle left), 5 (middle right), 8, 9 (botom); Eye Ubiquitous 5 (bottom right), 11, 13, 27 (Mike Alkins); Robert Harding 9 (top); John and Penny Hubley 14 (top); Hutchinson Library 3, 23 (bottom) Eric Ayrs; Impact 7 (bottom), 24 (bottom); James Davis 1, 10 (bottom), 17; Norton Studios, Trinidad 28; Panos 5 (left top), 6, 12 (top) Betty Press, 20; South American Pictures 21; St. Lucia Tourist Board 16, 26 (bottom); Trip 22 (T. Bogna), 12 (A. Tovey); (top) Zul Mukhida 14, 18, 26.

Books to Read

Anthony, Suzanne. *West Indies* (Major World Nations). New York: Chelsea House, 1998.

Brownlie, Alison. *Jamaica* (Country Insights). Austin, TX: Raintree Steck-Vaughn, 1998.

Haverstock, Nathan. *Dominican Republic in Pictures* (Visual Geography). Minneapolis, MN: Lerner Publications, 1997.

Hintz, Martin. *Haiti* (Enchantment of the World, Second Series). Danbury, CT: Children's Press, 1998.

Hodge, Alison. *The West Indies* (Country Fact Files). Austin, TX: Raintree Steck-Vaughn, 1998.

Mayer, T. W. *The Caribbean and Its People* (People and Places) Austin, TX: Thomson Learning, 1995.

Index

Page numbers in **bold** mean there is a photograph on the page.